How I Became A Socialist

Jack London

Jack London

Jack London was born in San Francisco, USA in 1876. In order to support his working class family, he left school at the age of fourteen and worked in a string of unskilled jobs, before returning briefly to graduate. Around this time, London discovered the public library in Oakland, and immersed himself in the literature of the day. In 1894, after a spell working on merchant ships, he set out to experience the life of the tramp, with a view to gaining an insight into the national class system and the raw essence of the human condition. At the age of nineteen, upon returning, London was admitted to the University of California in Berkeley, but left before graduating after just six months due to financial pressures.

London published his first short story, 'Typhoon off the Coast of Japan', in 1893. At this point, he turned seriously to writing, producing work at a prolific rate. Over the next decade, he began to be published in major magazines of the day, producing some of his best-remembered stories, such as 'To Build a Fire'. Starting in 1902, London turned to novels, producing almost twenty in fifteen years. Of these, his best-known are *Call of the Wild* and *White Fang*, both set during the Klondike Gold Rush. He also produced a number of popular and still widely-anthologized stories, such as 'An Odyssey of the North' and 'Love of Life'. London even proved himself as an excellent journalist, reporting on the 1906 earthquake in San Francisco and the Mexican Revolution of 1910.

London was an impassioned advocate of socialism and workers' rights, and these themes inform a number of his works – most notably his dystopian novel *The Iron Heel,* published in 1907. He even ran unsuccessfully as the Socialist nominee for mayor of Oakland on two occasions. London died in 1916, aged 40.

CONTENTS

Athol Books, 10 Athol Street, Belfast BT12
4GX, Northern Ireland.

First printing, July 1977
Second printing, June 1978

INTRODUCTION

Jack London and Nietzsche

Jack London is best known for his animal stories, White
Fang and The Call of the Wild, *"books which appealed to
the Anglo-Saxon sentimentality about animals"*, as George
Orwell put it. He is also known for his quite ferocious
story, Love of Life, in an introduction to which Orwell
made the foregoing comment. Love of Life was read to
Lenin as he was dying, and appealed to him very strongly.
It is the story of a wounded man painfully making his way
across the Arctic to keep an appointment with a ship. He
becomes aware that he is being stalked by a sick wolf, and
that the wolf is waiting for him to become weak enough to
pounce on. He adapts himself to the situation by stalking
the wolf in turn. Man and wolf see each other as food. And
it is the man who sinks his teeth in the wolf's throat.

The unconditional will to live is basic to London's writings.
It is what he expresses best. But his writings are, of
course, not a simple expression of the will to live. They
are literature about the will to live, they are the will to
live reflecting on itself and forging out of itself marketable
short stories and novels. It is therefore not at all para-

doxical that Jack London should have committed suicide.
It is one thing to survive an encounter with a wolf in
the Arctic by drinking its blood. It is quite a different thing to survive in the cultural milieu of California
as a successful writer on the primitive will to live.

It is not suggested that London was in any sense a fraud,
or that he was only acquainted as an observer with the
basic subject of his writings. He was born illegitimate
and poor, went to work in a factory at eleven, b/ecame a
working sailor at sixteen, and made his way in a tough world
by sheer strength and determination. He was in that respect
quite unlike Nietzsche, who had weak nerves, an absurdly
sensitive stomach, constant neurasthenia, and a most
cultured biography.

Jack London became a socialist *"in a fashion somewhat
similar to the way in which the Teutonic pagans became
Christians"* as he puts it in one of the articles reprinted
in this pamphlet. His best known socialist work is the
novel about counter-revolution in an advanced capitalist
society, The Iron Heel. This novel is in some respects an
anticipation of fascism. It is a unique work in socialist
literature. It was published in 1907 and took on a new
lease of literary life after 1933.

George Orwell's virtue was his ability to ask awkward
questions, and his insistence on asking them. This way-
ward characteristic gave him a greater affinity with Jack
London than any other recent writer has shown. Orwell
commented on The Iron Heel:

*"the book is chiefly notable for maintaining that capital-
ist society would not perish of its 'contradictions', but
that the possessing class would be able to form itself into a vast corporation and even evolve a sort of perverted
Socialism, sacrificing many of its privileges in order to
preserve its superior social status. The passages in
which London analyses the mentality of the Oligarchs are
of great interest:*

'They as a class believed that they alone maintained
civilisation...Without them, anarchy would reign and humanity would drop backward into the primitive night

2

out of which it had so painfully emerged...I cannot
lay too great stress upon this high ethical righteous-
ness of the whole Oligarch class. This has been the
strength of the Iron Heel, and too many of the
comrades have been slow or loath to realise it...
The great driving force of the Oligarchs is the
belief that they are doing right.'

*"From these and similar passages it can be seen that
London's understanding of the nature of a ruling class –
that is, the characteristics which a ruling class must
have if it is to survive – went very deep. According to
the conventional left-wing view, the 'Capitalist' is
simply a cynical scoundrel, without honour or courage,
and intent only on filling his own pockets. London knew
that this view was false. But why, one might justly ask,
should this hurried, sensational, in some ways childish
writer have understood that particular thing so much
better than the majority of his fellow Socialists?*

*"The answer is surely that London could foresee Fascism
because he had a Fascist streak in himself...His outlook
was democratic in the sense that he hated exploitation and
hereditary privilege, and that he felt most at home in the
company of people who worked with their hands: but his
instinct lay towards acceptance of a 'natural aristocracy'
of strength, beauty and talent. Intellectually he knew,
as one can see from various remarks in The Iron Heel, that
Socialism ought to mean the meek inheriting the earth, but
that was not what his temperament demanded. In much of
his work one strain in his character simply kills off the
other: he is at best when they interact"* (Introduction to
Love of Life, 1946)

In The People of the Abyss, (which has many points of
similarity with Orwell's Down and Out in Paris and London),
Jack London describes life amongst the lumpenproletariat
of the London East End in 1902. And London found what was
probably his most appreicative British readership in a
later generation of the lumpenproletariat. In the Rowton
Houses of Camden Town and Kings Cross about 1960 there was
a cultural elite to whom Jack London was well known and

amongst whom he was well understood. They appreciated
Orwell, but they appreciated London much more. It was not
just that London had written about an earlier generation of
themselves. Their interest in him went far beyond The
People of the Abyss. They appreciated his whole way of
looking at the world.

*"London was a Socialist with the instincts of a buccaneer
and the education of a 19th century materialist"*, according
to Orwell. And a generation of migrant Irish tramp
navvies and casual labourers, whose origins lay in the
thirties and forties, gave rise to a reflective cultural
group of that very kind. They could savour London, and
feel no need to impose moral harmony on him, or smooth
down the rough edges. They appreciated his ambiguity and
roughness no less than his other qualities.

Not everybody is aesthetically qualified to read the short
story called Semper Idem, and to savour it as beauty, as
"emotion recollected in tranquillity". It is about a doctor
who performs a remarkable operation to save a man who has
cut his throat from ear to ear. The operation was only
possible because the would-be suicide was looking down at
a photograph of a woman when committing the act. This had
the effect of bunching up the muscles of his throat to resist the slash of the razor. When the man was being dis-
charged the surgeon, who had taken a keen interest in him,
offered him a bit of friendly advice: *"Next time you try
it on, hold your chin up, so. Don't snuggle it down and
butcher yourself like a cow. Neatness and despatch, you
know. Neatness and despatch."* The next day, the man,
who never utters a word in the course of the story, is
back in the hospital with his throat properly cut.

Such stories might have formal similarities with the sick
humour of more recent times, but the atmosphere is quite
different. They are told in a different spirit.
                                    ****

In The Iron Heel, the narrator describes her first im-
pression of the hero, Ernest Everard: *"He was a natural
aristocrat - and this in spite of the fact that he was
in the camp of the non-aristocrats. He was a superman,*

4

*a blond beast such as Nietzsche has described, and in
addition he was aflame with democracy".* The novel is
supposed to be a manuscript discovered many centuries
hence, and includes footnotes by a supposed Editor.
There is a footnote at this point: *"Friedrich Nietzsche,
the mad philosopher of the 19th century...who caught
wild glimpses of truth, but who, before he was done,
reasoned himself around the great circle of human thought
and off into madness."*

Biographies of London tend to be tedious affairs. The
wrong people write them. It is very easy to be the wrong
person to write the biography of Jack London.

The question of Nietzsche is one great difficulty con-
fronting the biographer. London was a socialist offspring
of Marx and Nietzsche. His world outlook developed through
a cross fertilisation of The Communist Manifesto and Thus
Spake Zarathustra.

This awkward genealogy is dealt with as follows in a
biography by Richard O'Connor, published by Gollancz in
1965:

*"But it was Friedrich Nietzsche's deep dark well of
pessimism at which he drank most copiously. The embittered German philosopher...seemed to confirm and
enlarge upon so much of what he had learned from experience. 'I teach you the Superman. Man is something
to be surpassed...' From his early teens he had regarded
himself as a superior creature, one born to dominate his
fellows because he was stronger and wiser. This belief
existed side by side, uneasily and incongruously, with
his fervent dedication to Socialism which was supposed to
protect the weaker and more ignorant.*

*"His own anti-religious beliefs were given substance by
Nietzsche's tirade against Christianity:* 'I call Christianity the one great curse, the one enormous and innermost
perversion, the one great instinct of revenge, for which
no means are too venomous, too underhand, or too petty –
I call it the one immoral blemish of mankind.' *Or:* 'After

5

coming into contact with the religious I must wash my hands...' *Even his flirtation with suicide found a certain amount of confirmation in the German:* 'The thought of suicide is a great consolation; by means of it one gets through many a bad night'. *Throughout his life Jack held that death was final and man was obliterated by it as completely as a casually swatted mosquito...*

"*Yet he would also say that of all men who ever lived Jesus Christ was one of the two whom he admired most; Abraham Lincoln was the other. The mutually exclusive held no terrors for Jack London. He could be an atheist who valued the example of Christ, a Socialist who believed in the levelling process of revolution at the same time he raised up an image of the Superman who would rightfully dominate the stupid herd. Even in his worst nightmares, however, he would hardly have conceived that the self-appointed Superman who finally arose from the Nietzschean compost-pile would be an Adolf Hitler*". (pp 121-122)

If "*the mutually exclusive held no terrors for Jack London*", then he was a true Nietzschean. Nietzsche tended towards the epigram as his ideal literary style, and he deliberately refrained from arguing his epigrams into a consistent system of thought. If two epigrams were inconsistent with each other, and yet each of them seemed to be true, so be it. He did not value harmony at the expense of truth.

O'Connor only quotes one of Nietzsche's ideas about religion. As far as that idea goes, it must be said that Nietzsche is far from being the only person who felt an ' urge to cleanse himself after contact with the much-washed hands of the priest, or who regarded religion as a dark, venomous and vindictive force.

Nietzsche's other idea about the Jewish/Christian religion is that it signified a "*slave revolt in morals*", and that it was through the priesthood that the subjective side of humanity developed into a subject of infinite interest to humanity. Kant pointed out that, in addition to infinity outside man, there was an infinity within him. He philos-

ophised ahistorically about the infinity within. Nietzsche
tried to explain how the infinity within had developed in
history. Therefore Kant is a very proper sort of philosopher and moralist, while Nietzsche is very improper.

Nietzsche regarded Jesus as the great degenerate. A degenerate in the Nietzschean sense is best understood by
reference to his opposite, a person who confirms the
values of his time and his society. The degenerate does
the contrary of this. Development is therefore bound up
with degeneracy.

Nietzsche was anything but an *"embittered German philosopher"*. The German philosophers from Kant to Nietzsche
were absolutely enthralled by themselves, so how could
they be embittered? Most of them went in for a profound
literary style, so their good humour might not be
immediately apparent. But Nietzsche went in for brevity
and transparency of literary style. It is very remarkable
that he should be so widely thought to have been embittered.
His nastiest comments and his most *'pessimistic'* reflections were all uttered in a mood of sprightly good humour.
Even his ridiculously delicate constitution was a matter
of great interest to himself. He marvelled at his entire
existence. When he said that the thought of suicide
was a consolation on many a bad night he was not being
bitter, he was passing an interesting remark about himself.

He is best known as the philosopher of the will to power,
though he published very little on the subject. A large
volume of bits and pieces was published under the title,
The Will to Power, by his sister after he went mad. His
sister married one of the leaders of the anti-Semitic
strain in German nationalism, and, as the possessor of
his remains and guardian of his memory, fabricated a
connection between Nietzsche and anti-Semitic nationalism.
But in Nietzsche's writings what one finds is a profound
admiration for the Jews, and continuous sneering at German
nationalism. (*"The Germans have no fingers, they have only
paws"*, should satisfy the most demanding taste.)

7

There is a brief passage on the will to power in Zarathustra: *"I have crept into the very heart of life and into the roots of its heart. And wherever I found a living thing, there I found a will to power; and even in the will of those that serve I found the will to be master. The weaker serves the stronger: it is persuaded to do so by its own will, which would be master over what is weaker still...And where men make sacrifices and serve and cast amorous glances, there too is the will to be master."*

This appears in the section, On Self-Overcoming, along with other reflections such as: *"Wherever I found a living thing, there I found talk on obedience. Whatever lives, obeys. And in the second place, he who cannot obey himself is commanded...There is however a third point: that commanding is harder than obeying; and this is not only because he who commands must carry the buden of all who obey and that burden may easily crush him...When a living thing commands, it hazards itself. Even when it commands itself, it must pay for commanding. It must become the judge, the executioner and the victim of its own law. How can this happen? I ask myself. What induces a living being to obey and command, and to practice obedience even when it commands?"* And he finds an answer in the convolutions of the will to power. The cruder expressions of the will to power, the blond beasts, only interested him superficially and briefly.

In the age of psychology and psychiatry, which set in a few years after Nietzsche's death, it is remarkable that such reflections as those quoted should be found shocking, or even slightly distrubing. His bad reputation would be understandable if he had used the notion of the will to power to glorify or justify the German state, ruling class or social condition. He did no such thing. In his peculiar autobiography, Ecce Homo, (and is not an autobiography deceptive which is not peculiar?), he boasts quite truthfully: *"I only attack causes which are victorious - and at times I wait until they are victorious...I attack only causes against which I cannot expect to find allies."* With every book he isolated himself still further from the trend of events in

8

Germany. He had a small private income with which he published small editions of his books of which only a small number sold: ten or twenty in some cases. In his own life he exhibited a most rarefied convolution of the will to power.

The fact is that the notorious philosopher of the will to power was scarcely interested in power in the customary sense. His obsession was with something else entirely: *"This unconditional will to truth: what is it?"* He had a compulsion to ask awkward questions and to try to answer them regardless of the consequences. And the question of how that could be is what fascinated him.

Awkward questions about morality were what preoccupied him most. In The Genealogy of Morals, *"the object is to explore the huge, distant and thoroughly hidden country of morality, morality as it has actually existed and actually been lived..."* He sets out to unravel the history of morals. But if morality is a product of historical evolution, a history of morality must be immoral. A moral historian will fake the history of morals in order that it will be uplifting. A historian who is impelled by the *"unconditional will to truth"* will try to discover what actually happened in the evolution of morals. And what is the will to truth which is prepared to undermine morality?

"Stoning...; breaking on the wheel...; piercing with stakes, drawing and quartering, trampling to death with horses, boiling in oil or wine, the popular flaying alive, cutting out of flesh from the chest, smearing the victim with honey and leaving him in the sun, a prey to flies. By such methods the individual was finally taught to remember five or six 'I won't.'s which entitled him to the benefits of society; and indeed, with the aid of this sort of memory, people eventually 'came to their esnses'. What an enormous price man had to pay for reason, seriousness, control over his emotions – those grand human prerogatives and cultural showpieces! How much blood and horror lies behind all 'good things'!"

9

This is a far cry from Kant's *"categorical imperative"*, that pure emanation from the transcendental world.

Perhaps Nietzsche helped to make the more outrageous forms of Nazi behaviour possible by treating morality as a product of history. If so, every trend in materialist philosophy which helped to undermine Christianity also contributed. However, Nietzsche did not think of himself as a warrior against God, but as a person to whom certain awkward questions occurred because he realised that God was dead.

"Pity is the practice of nihilism...It multiplies misery and conserves all that is miserable, and is thus a prime instrument of the advancement of decadence: pity persuades men to nothingness...In our whole unhealty modernity there is nothing more unhealthy than Christian pity" (The Anti-Christ). This is the sort of thing that gives Nietzsche a bad odour. But he is far from being unique in holding such a view. Other philosophers hav e held it. The difference is that they held it with a more matter-of-fact brutality. Indeed, in the Christian era, the Church itself was most sparing in the practice of pity in any tangible form. The trouble with Nietzsche was that he was far too honest and sensitive a soul to cope with the unconditional will to truth, and made a great fuss when he discovered something unpleasant. He looked down on the sentimentality of the English philosophers: but their sentimentality concealed a toughness that he was constitutionally incapable of.

A few months after writing The Anti-Christ he took pity on a horse that was being flogged by a coachman, threw his' arms around it to protect it, went mad, and declared himself to be Jesus Christ. But even his madness was interesting. He explained, in his last letter, how reluctant he had been to become God: *"In the end I would much rather be a Basel professor than God; but I have not dared push my private egoism so far as to desist for its sake from the creation of the world. You see, one must make sacrifices however and wherever one lives"* (Letter to Jacob Burckhardt. January 6, 1889).   ****

10

Nietzsche went mad at the moment when his most interesting successor was getting into his stride. This successor emerged unexpectedly from the working class, about which Nietzsche had only the haziest idea. He wrote a paragraph on *"The labour question"* in The Twilight of the Idols, which only expresses puzzlement: *"The stupidity... is that there is a labour question at all...I simply cannot see what one proposes to do with the European worker now that one has made a question of him. He is far too well off not to ask for more, and not to ask more immodestly. In the end, he has numbers on his side. The hope is gone forever that a modest and self-sufficient kind of man, a Chinese type, might here develop as a class: and there would have been reason in that...But what was done? Everything to nip in the bud even the preconditions for this: the instincts by virtue of which the worker becomes possible as a class, possible in his own eyes, have been destroyed through and through with the most irresponsible thoughtlessness. The worker was qualified for military service, granted the right to organise and to vote: is it any wonder that the worker today experiences his own existence as an injustice? But what is wanted? I ask once more. If one wants an end, one must also want the means: if one wants slaves, then one is a fool if one educates them to be masters."*

This passage has at least the virtue of recognising that the modern proletariat differed from all previous lower classes in that it would be unlikely to reproduce itself contentedly, (or, if not contentedly, resignedly), on an indefinite basis. The most acute writer of epigrams, when read three quarters of a century later, will tend to miss as often as he hits. But the observation that the modern worker *"experiences his own existence as an injustice"* has gained in relevance with the passage of time. He might have gone on to reflect that a class whose very existence constitutes a problem for itself and for every other part of society must be a profoundly interesting phenomenon. It is therefore not surprising that the only worthy successor of Nietzsche emerged in the process of development of the working class. Hordes of petty bourgeois intellectuals began to imitate him shortly after his death. They aspired to be the soul of indiscretion, but were merely tedious since they had nothing of substance to be indiscrete about.

"I called him an abysmal brute, and he never forgave me. Yet I meant it as a compliment". There is a true Nietzschean ring to that sort of statement. It came naturally to Jack London, while it evaded a horde of intellectuals who beat the air trying to produce it.

Captain Wolf Larsen in The Sea Wolf is usually considered to be London's most Nietzschean creation. *("...life is a mess. It is like yeast, a ferment, a thing that moves and may move for a minute, an hour, a year, a hundred years, but that in the end will cease to move. The big eat the little that they may continue to move, the strong eat the weak that they may retain their strength. The lucky eat the most and move the longest.")* In fact that only represents the more superficial side of the Nietzschean view.

That notorious literary product, The Yellow Peril, is regarded as an indefensible expression by London of Nietzschean racism. In fact, neither Nietzsche nor London were distinguished by their racism.

It is only in recent times that it has come to be generally agreed that racial differences have no social significance, and that cultural differences have nothing to do with race. Prior to the age of capitalist imperialism racial differences were generally assumed to be of importance socially. The scientific conflict about the race question was in fact a process in which naive racism was overcome, and the racist outlook was proved to be delusory in the attempt to develop it as a science. Nietzsche and London flirted with racist ideas in the way that they flirted with every other question of the age, and their flirtations are memorable only because they made everything they touched more vivid. They were not systematic racists.

12

London is at his most Nietzschean in The War of the
Classes, from which the articles reprinted here have
been taken. In How I Became a Socialist he recounts how
the blond beast became civilised; and in the New Law of
Development he raises an awkward question about civilisation: The survival of the fittest has been the law of
development hitherto: how will development contrive to
take place if this law is negated by socialism?

No attempt will be made to answer that awkward question
in this Introduction, but it might be of interest to say
a few words about its history. Nietzsche set out to
challenge *"the retarding influence which democratic
prejudice has had upon all investigations of origins"*,
and he produced his scandalous history of morals. He
asked the dangerous question: *"What if morality should
turn out to be the danger of dangers?"* In Zarathustra,
he tried to envisage the social consequence of a com-
prehensive egalitarian morality, which equated effort
with pain, and he came up with *"the last man"*.

*"Alas, the time is coming when man will no longer shoot
the arrow of his longing beyond man...I say unto you: one
must still have chaos within oneself to be able to give
birth to a dancing star. I say unto you: you still have
chaos in yourselves. Alas, the time is coming when man
will no longer give birth to a star. Alas, the time of
the most despicable man is coming, he that is no longer
able to despise himself. Behold, I show you the last man.*

*"'What is love? What is creation? What is longing? What
is a star?' thus asks the last man, and he blinks. The
earth has become small...and on it hops the last man, who
makes everything small. His race is as ineradicable as
the flea-beetle; the last man lives longest. 'We have*

13

*invented happiness', say the last men, and they blink...
One still loves one's neighbour and rubs against him, for
one needs warmth. Becoming sick and harbouring suspicion
are sinful to them: one proceeds carefully...A little
poison now and then: that makes for agreeable dreams. And
much poison in the end, for an agreeable death. One still
works, for work is a form of entertainment. But one is
careful lest the entertainment be too harrowing. One no
longer becomes rich or poor: both require too much exertion.
No shepherd and one herd! Everybody wants to be the same,
everybody is the same: whoever feels differently goes
voluntarily into a madhouse. 'Formerly, all the world was
mad', say the most refined, and they blink. One has one's
little pleasures for the day and one's little pleasures for
the night: but one has regard to health. 'We have invented
happiness' say the last men, and they blink".*

A few years ago this horrible thought about the last men
seemed to be coming true in the shape of gentle people
with flowers in their hair. (And it then became apparent
that what Nietzsche failed to realise is that the last
men would only overcome their turbulence by involuting it
into bitchiness.) But today that prospect has receded.

It is sometimes assumed that the last men found their
fullest expression in the socialist movement. But while
there are of course last men amongst the socialists, they
are only the bourgeois heritage of socialism. The working
class movement is not a producer of last men. It erodes
and devalues the individuality of other classes in the process of developing individuality within itself. And the
Bolshevik revolution produces the polar opposite of the
last men, as well as bearing out the conception of the
amoral means by which morals and ideals become substantial.
(*"Would anyone care to learn something about the way in
which ideals are manufactured? Does anyone have the
nerve?"* Read The Gulag Archipelago.)

If one looks around for the preachers of the last man
today, one finds them in Margaret Thatcher and Keith
Joseph. The individuality which they preach is miserable,

14

superficial, ignoble, and it is all of these things because it is bereft of power. Theirs is not the individualism of people who pursue power and are confident in the use of power: it is the individualism of an obsolescent class which seeks holes and corners in which to hide itself from a terrible and irresistible will to power that is grinding it into dust.

A capitalist class which only aspires to tolerance in a *"social market economy"*, and which is therefore only motivated by the meanest considerations of personal gain, is not a soil in which the Nietzschean spirit can flourish. The bourgeois Nietzschean only fantasises.

The *"slave revolt in morals"* which fascinated Nietzsche, has now developed into the most substantial will to power. The socialist movement is now the only place where the Nietzschean spirit can develop in a substantial manner. Of course there will never be a specific Nietzschean tendency in the socialist movement. His writings are too unsystematic, (and deliberately so), to allow that to be possible. But there is undoubtedly a Nietzschean streak within Communism.

The most obvious expression of this was Trotsky. But Trotsky was only the most obvious Nietzschean because he expressed the most vulgar aspect of Nietzscheanism. Trotsky in 1923/4 is a fascinating figure. In 1917-22 he was the exhibitionist superman of the revolution, directing the "masses" and speaking their mind for them most eloquently. Then in 1923-4 he found himself almost amongst the masses. Elements from amongst the masses had risen into the ruling oligarchy during the civil war, and it was necessary that the oligarchy should be most intimately concerned with the mass of the people through a system of *"transmission belts"* as Lenin put it) if it was to govern effectively. Trotsky's personal relationship with the masses changed. When he stood above them and shaped them and uttered noble thoughts on their behalf, they were in the nature of an ideal, or even an idea, for him. But when he began to mix with them, when communication with them was no longer a simple matter of speaking on their behalf - then he held

his nose in disgust, like Zarathustra amongst the rabble.
(In <u>Literature And Revolution</u> he remarked that Nietzsche
had contributed something of value to aesthetics. He
didn't explain what it was. Since that book was written
during the Civil War he could not yet know about his
aesthetic affinity with Zarathustra before the latter
overcame his nausea.)

Nietzschean vulgarity has one spectacular figure in the
socialist movement to exemplify it. The better features
of the Nietzschean spirit are not so sharply defined or
clearly exemplified. Suffice it to say that a Communist
who reads Nietzsche will find much that is not incomprehen-
sible or alien to him, and that the fuss that has been made
about the Nietzschean aspect of Jack London is unwarranted.

London died of a drug overdose in 1916. Shortly before he
died he wrote a letter of resignation to the Socialist
Party, *"because of its lack of fire and fight, and its
loss of emphasis on the class struggle".*

*"I was originally a member of the old revolutionary, upon-
its-hind-legs, fighting Socialist Labour Party...Since the
whole trend of Socialism in the United States during recent
years has been one of peaceableness and compromise, I find
that my mind refuses further sanction of my remaining a
party member...*

*"My final word is that liberty, freedom and independence,
are royal things that cannot be presented to, nor thrust
upon, races or classes. If faces and classes cannot rise
up and by their strength of brawn and brain, wrest from
the world liberty, freedom and independence...,they never
can come to these royal possessions...and if such things
are kindly presented to them by superior individuals, on
silver platters, they will not know what to do with them,
will fail to make use of them, and will be what they have
always been in the past...inferior races and classes."*

If he had hung on for another year, he would have found
life interesting again.

BRITISH & IRISH COMMUNIST
ORGANISATION. July 1977.

HOW I BECAME A SOCIALIST

IT is quite fair to say that I became a Socialist
in a fashion somewhat similar to the way in which the Teutonic pagans became Christians - it was hammered into me. Not
only was I not looking for Socialism at the time of my conversion, but I was fighting it. I was very young and
callow, did not know much of anything, and though I had
never even heard of a school called "Individualism", I
sang the paean of the strong with all my heart.

This was because I was strong myself. By strong I
mean that I had good health and hard muscles, both of which
possession are easily accounted for. I had lived my child-
hood on California ranches, my boyhood hustling newspapers
on the streets of a healthy Western city, and my youth on
the ozone-laden waters of San Francisco Bay and the Pacific
Ocean. I loved life in the open, and I toiled in the open,
at the hardest kinds of work. Learning no trade, but
drifting along from job to job, I looked on the world and
called it good, every bit of it. Let me repeat, this
optimism was because I was healthy and strong, bothered
with neither aches nor weaknesses, never turned down by
the boss because I did not look fit, able always to get
a job at shovelling coal, sailorizing, or manual labour
of some sort.

And because of this, exulting in my young life, able
to hold my own at work or fight, I was a rampant individualist. It was very natural, I was a winner. Wherefore I
called the game, as I saw it played, or thought I saw it
played, a very proper game for MEN. To be a MAN was to
write man in large capitals on my heart. To adventure like
a man, and fight like a man, and do a man's work (even for
a boy's pay) - these were things that reached right in and
gripped hold of me as no other thing could. And I looked
ahead into long vistas of a hazy and interminable future,

17

into which, playing what I conceived to be MAN's game, I should continue to travel with unfailing health, without accidents, and with muscles ever vigorous. As I say, this future was interminable. I could see myself only raging through life without end like one of Nietzsche's *blond beasts*, lustfully roving and conquering by sheer superiority and strength.

As for the unfortunates, the sick, and ailing, and old, and maimed, I must confess I hardly thought of them at all, save that I vaguely felt that they, barring accidents could be as good as I if they wanted to real hard, and could work just as well. Accidents? Well, they represented FATE, also spelled out in capitals, and there was no getting around FATE. Napoleon had had an accident at Waterloo, but that did not dampen my desire to be another and later Napoleon. Further, the optimism bred of a stomach which could digest scrap iron and a body which flourished on hardships did not permit me to consider accidents as even remotely related to my glorious personality.

I hope I have made it clear that I was proud to be one of Nature's strong-armed noblemen. The dignity of labor was to me the most impressive thing in the world. Without having read Carlyle, or Kipling, I formulated a gospel of work which put theirs in the shade. Work was everything. It was sanctification and salvation. The pride I took in a hard day's work well done would be inconceivable to you. It is almost inconceivable to me as I look back upon it. I was as faithful a wage slave as ever capitalist exploited. To shirk or malinger on the man who paid me my wages was a sin, first, against myself, and second, against him. I considered it a crime second only to treason and just about as bad.

In short, my joyous individualism was dominated by the orthodox bourgeois ethics. I read the bourgeois papers, listened to the bourgeois preachers, and shouted at the sonorous platitudes of the bourgeois politicians. And I

doubt not, if other events had not changed my career, that
I should have evolved into a professional strike-breaker,
(one of President Eliot's American heroes), and had my
head and my earning power irrevocably smashed by a club
in the hands of some militant trades-unionist.

Just about this time, returning from a seven months'
voyage before the mast, and just turned eighteen, I took
it into my head to go tramping. On rods and blind baggages
I fought my way from the open West, where men bucked big and
the job hunted the man, to the congested labor centres of
the East, where men were small potatoes and hunted the job
for all they were worth. And on this new *blond-beast* adventure I found myself looking upon life from a new and totally
different angle. I had dropped down from the proletariat
into what sociologists love to call the "submerged tenth",
and I was startled to discover the way in which that submerged tenth was recruited.

I found there all sorts of men, many of whom had once
been as good as myself and just as *blond-beastly*; sailor-
men, soldier-men, labor-men, all wrenched and distorted and
twisted out of shape by toil and hardship and accident, and
cast adrift by their masters like so many old horses. I
battered on the drag and slammed back gates with them, or
shivered with them in box cars and city parks, listening
the while to life-histories which began under auspices as
fair as mine, with digestions and bodies equal to and
better than mine, and which ended there before my eyes in
the shambles at the bottom of the Social Pit.

And as I listened my brain began to work. The
woman of the streets and the man of the gutter drew very
close to me. I saw the picture of the Social Pit as vividly
as though it were a concrete thing, and at the bottom of the
Pit I saw them, myself above them, not far, and hanging on
to the slippery wall by main strength and sweat. And I
confess a terror seized me. What when my strength failed?
when I should be unable to work shoulder to shoulder with

19

the strong men who were as yet babes unborn? And there and
then I swore a great oath. It ran something like this: *All
my days I have worked hard with my body, and according to
the number of days I have worked, by just that much am I
nearer the bottom of the Pit. I shall climb out of the Pit,
but not by the muscles of my body shall I climb out. I
shall do no more hard work, and may God strike me dead if
I do another day's hard work with my body more than I absolutely have to do.* And I have been buy ever since running
away from hard work.

Incidentally, while tramping some ten thousand miles
through the United States and Canada, I strayed into
Niagara Falls, was nabbed by a fee-hunting constable,
denied the right to plead guilty or not guilty, sentenced
out of hand to thirty days' imprisonment for having no
fixed abode and no visible means of support, handcuffed
and chained to a bunch of men similarly circumstanced,
carted down country to Buffalo, registered at the Erie
County Penitentiary, had my head clipped and my budding
mustache shaved, was dressed in convict stripes, com-
pulsorily vaccinated by a medical student who practised
on such as we, made to march the lock-step, and put to work
under the eye of guards armed with Winchester rifles - all
for adventuring in *blond-beastly* fashion. Concerning
further details deponent sayeth not, though he may hint
that some of his plethoric national patriotism simmered
down and leaked out of the bottom of his soul somewhere
- at least, since that experience he finds that he cares
more for men and women and little children than for imag-
inary geographical lines.

To return to my conversion. I think it is apparent
that my rampant individualism was pretty effectively
hammered out of me, and something else as effectively
hammered in. But just as I had been an individualist
without knowing it, I was now a Socialist without knowing it, withal, an unscientific one. I had been reborn,

but not renamed, and I was running around to find out
what manner of thing I was. I ran back to California
and opened the books. I do not remember which ones I
opened first. It is an unimportant detail anyway. I
was already It, whatever It was, and by aid of the books
I discovered It was a Socialist. Since that day I have
opened many books, but no economic argument, no lucid
demonstration of the logic and inevitableness of Socialism affects me as profoundly and convincingly as I was
affected on the day when I first saw the walls of the
Social Pit rise around me and felt myself slipping down,
down, into the shambles at the bottom.

WANTED:
A NEW LAW OF DEVELOPMENT

EVOLUTION is no longer a mere tentative hypothesis.
One by one, step by step, each division and sub-division
of science has contributed its evidence, until now the
case is complete and the verdict is rendered. While there
is still discussion as to the method of evolution, none the
less, as a process sufficient to explain all biological
phenomena, all differentiations of life into widely diverse
species, families, and even dkingdoms, evolution is flatly
accepted. Likewise has been accepted its law of development:
*That, in the struggle for existence, the strong and fit and
the progeny of the strong and fit have a better opportunity
for survival than the weak and less fit and the progeny of
the weak and less fit.*

It is in the struggle of the species with other species
and against all other hostile forces in the environment,
that this law operates; also in the struggle between the
individuals of the same species. In this struggle, which
is for food and shelter, the weak individuals must obviously
win less food and shelter than the strong. Because of this,
their hold on life relaxes and they are eliminated. And
for the same reason that they may not win for themselves
adequate food and shelter, the weak cannot give to their
progeny the chance for survival that the strong give. And
thus, since the weak are prone to beget weakness, the species
is constantly purged of its inefficient members.

Because of this, a premium is placed upon strength,
and so long as the struggle for food and shelter obtains,
just so long will the average strength of each generation
increase. On the other hand, should conditions so change
that all, and the progeny of all, the weak as well as the
strong, have an equal chance for survival, then at once,
the average strength of each generation will begin to

diminish. Never yet, however, in animal life, has there
been such a state of affairs. Natural selection has always
obtained. The strong and their progeny at the expense of
the weak, have always survived. This law of development
has operated down all the past upon all life; so it operates
to-day, and it is not rash to say that it will continue to
operate in the future - at least upon all life existing in
a state of nature.

Man, pre-eminent though he is in the animal kingdom,
capable of reacting upon and making suitable an unsuitable
environment, nevertheless remains the creature of this same
law of development. The social selection to which he is
subject is merely another form of natural selection. True,
within certain narrow limits he modifies the struggle for
existence and renders less precarious the tenure of life
for the weak. The extremely weak, diseased, and inefficient are housed in hospitals and asylums. The strength
of the viciously strong, when inimical to society, is
tempered by penal institutions and by the gallows. The
short-sighted are provided with spectacles, and the sickly
(when they can pay for it) with sanitariums. Pestilential
marshes are drained, plagues are checked, and disasters
averted. Yet, for all that, the strong and the progeny
of the strong survive, and the weak are crushed out. The
men strong of brain are masters as of yore. They dominate
society and gather to themselves the wealth of society.
With this wealth they maintain themselves and equip their
progeny for the struggle. They build their homes in
healthful places, purchase the best fruits,,meats, and
vegetables the market affords, and buy themselves the min-
istrations of the most brilliant and learned of the professional classes. The weak man, as of yore, is the serv-
ant, the doer of things at the master's call. The weaker
and less efficient he is, the poorer is his regard. The
weakest work for a living wage, (when they can get work),
live in insanitary slums, on vile and insufficient food,
at the lowest depths of human degradation. Their grasp
on life is indeed precarious, their mortality excessive,
their infant death-rate appalling.

That some should be born to preferment and others to
ignominy in order that the race may progress, is cruel and
sad; but none the less they are so born. The weeding out
of human souls, some for fatness and smiles, some for
leanness and tears, is surely a heartless selective process - as heartless as it is natural. And the human
family, for all its wonderful record of adventure and
achievement, has not yet succeeded in avoiding this process. That it is incapable of doing this is not to be
hazarded. Not only is it capable, but the whole trend
of society is in that direction. All the social forces
are driving man on to a time when the old selective
law will be annulled. There is no escaping it, save by
the intervention of catastrophes and cataclysms quite
unthinkable. It is inexorable. It is inexorable because the common man demands it. The twentieth century,
the common man says, is his day; the common man's day,
or rather, the dawning of the common man's day.

Nor can it be denied. The evidence is with him.
The previous centuries, and more notably the nineteenth,
have marked the rise of the common man. From chattel
slavery to serfdom, and from serfdom to what he bitterly
terms "wage slavery", he has risen. Never was he so
strong as he is to-day, and never so menacing. He does
the work of the world, and he is beginning to know it.
The world cannot get along without him, and this also he
is beginning to know. All the human knowledge of the
past, all the scientific discovery, governmental experim-
ent, and invention of machinery have tended to his advancement. His standard of living is higher. His common
school education would shame princes ten centuries past.
His civil and religious liberty makes him a free man, and
his ballot the peer of his betters. And all this has tended to make him conscious, conscious of himself, conscious
of his class. He looks about him and questions that
ancient law of development. It is cruel and wrong, he is
beginning to declare. It is an anachronism. Let it be
abolished. Why should there be one empty belly in the

24

world, when the work of ten men can feed a hundred?
What if my brother be not so strong as I? He has not
sinned. Wherefore should he hunger - he and his sinless
little ones? Away with the old law. There is food and
shelter for all, therefore let all receive food and
shelter.

As far as labor has become conscious it has organized.
The ambition of these class-conscious men is that the movement shall become general, that all labor shall become
conscious of itself and its class interests. And the
day that witnesses the solidarity of labor, they triumphantly affirm, will be a day when labor dominates the
world. This growing consciousness has led to the
organization of two movements, both separate and distinct,
but both converging toward a common goal - one, the
labor movement, known as Trade Unionism; the other, the
political movement, known as Socialism. Both are grim
and silent forces, unheralded and virtually unknown to
the general public save in moments of stress. The sleep-
ing labor giant receives little notice from the capitalistic press, and when he stirs uneasily, a column of surprise,
indignation, and horror suffices.

It is only now and then, after long periods of
silence, that the labor movement put in its claim for
notice. All is quite. The kind old world spins on,
and the bourgeois masters clip their coupons in smug
complacency. But the grim and silent forces are at
work. Suddenly, like a clap of thunder from a clear sky,
comes a disruption of industry. From ocean to ocean
the wheels of a great chain of railroads cease to run.
A quarter of a million miners throw down pick and shovel
and outrage the sun with their pale, bleached faces.
The street railways of a swarming metropolis stand idle,
or the rumble of machinery in vast manufactories dies
away to silence. There is alam and panic. Arson and
homicide stalk forth. There is a cry in the night, and
quick anger and sudden death. Peaceful cities are affrighted
by the crack of rifles and the snarl of machine-guns, and

the hearts of the shuddering are shaken by the roar of
dynamite. There is hurrying and skurrying. The wires are
kept hot between the centre of government and the seat of
trouble. The chiefs of state ponder gravely and advise,
and governors of states implore. There is assembling of
militia and massing of troops, and the streets resound to
the tramp of armed men. There are separate and joint
conferences between the captains of industry and the captains
of labor. And then, finally, all is quiet again, and the
memory of it is like the memory of a bad dream.

But these strikes become olympaids, things to date
from; and common on the lips of men become such phrases
as "The Great Dock Strike", "The Great Coal Strike",
"The Great Railroad Strike". Never before did labor do
these things. After the Great Plague in England, labor,
finding itself in demand and innocently obeying the economic law, asked higher wages. But the masters set a maximum
wage, restrained working men from moving about from place
to place, refused to tolerate idlers, and by most barbarous
legal methods punished those who disobeyed. But labor is
accorded greater respect to-day. Such a policy, put into
effect in this the first decade of the twentieth century,
would sweep the masters from their seats in one mighty
crash. And the masters know it and are respectful.

A fair instance of the growing solidarity of labor is
afforded by an unimportant recent strike in San Francisco.
The restaurant cooks and waiters were completely unorganised
working at any and all hours for whatever wages they could
get. A representative of the American Federation of Labor
went among them and organized them. Within a few weeks
nearly two thousand men were enrolled, and they had five
thousand dollars on deposit. Then they put in their demand
for increased wages and shorter hours. Forthwith their employers organized. The demand was denied, and the Cooks'
and Waiter' Union walked out.

26

All organized employers stood back of the restaurant owners, in sympathy with them and willing to aid them if they dared. And at the back of the Cooks' and Waiters' Union stood the organized labor of the city, 40,000 strong. If a business man was caught patronizing an "unfair" restaurant, he was boycotted; if a union man was caught, he was fined heavily by his union or expelled. The oyster companies and the slaughter houses made an attempt to refuse to sell oysters and meat to union restaurants. The Butchers and Meat Cutters, and the Teamsters, in retaliation, refused to work for or to deliver to non-union restaurants. Upon this the oyster companies and slaughter houses acknowledged themselves beaten and peace reigned. But the Restaurant Bakers in non-union places were ordered out, and the Bakery Wagon Drivers declined to deliver to unfair houses.

Every American Federation of Labor union in the city was prepared to strike, and waited only the word. And behind all, a handful of men, known as the Labor Council, directed the fight. One by one, blow upon blow, they were able if they deemed it necessary to call out the unions - the Laundry Workers, who do the washing; the Hackmen, who haul men to and from restaurants; the Butchers, Meat Cutters and Teamsters; and the Milkers, Milk Drivers, and Chicken Pickers; and after that, in pure sympathy, the Retail Clerks, the Horse Shoers, the Gas and Electrical Fixture Hangers, the Metal Roofers, the Blacksmiths, the Blacksmiths' Helpers, the Stablemen, the Machinists, the Brewers, the Coast Seamen, the Varnishers and Polishers, the Confectioners, the Upholsterers, the Paper Hangers and Fresco Painters, the Drug Clerks, the Fitters and Helpers, the Metal Workers, the Boiler Makers and Iron Ship Builders, the Assistant Undertakers, the Carriage and Wagon Workers, and so on down the lengthy list of organizations.

For, over all these trades, over all these thousands of men, is the Labor Council. When it speaks its voice is heard, and when it orders it is obeyed. But it, in turn,

is dominated by the National Labor Council, with which
it is constantly in touch. In this wholly unimportant
little local strike it is of interest to note the stands
taken by the different sides. The legal representative
and official mouthpiece of the Employers' Association
said: *"This organization is formed for defensive purposes,
and it may be driven to take offensive steps, and if so,
will be strong enough to follow them up. Labor cannot
be allowed to dictate to capital and say how business
shall be conducted. There is no objection to the format-
ion of unions and trades councils, but membership must
not be compulsory. It is repugnant to the American idea
of liberty and cannot be tolerated."*

On the other hand, the president of the Team Drivers'
Union said: *"The employers of labor in this city are
generally against the trade-union movement, and there
seemed to be a concerted effort on their part to check
the progress of organized labor. Such action as has
been taken by them in sympathy with the present labor
troubles may, if continued, lead to a serious conflict,
the outcome of which might be most calamitous for the
business and industrial interests of San Francisco."*

And the secretary of the United Brewery Workmen:
*I regard a sympathetic strike as the last weapon which
organized labor should use in its defence. When, however,
associations of employers band together to defeat
organized labor, or one of its branches, then we should
not and will not hesitate ourselves to employ the same
instrument in retaliation."*

Thus, in a little corner of the world, is exemplified
the growing solidarity of labor. The organization of
labor has not only kept pace with the organization of
industry, but it has gained upon it. In one winter, in
the anthracite coal region, $160,000 in mines and
$600,000,000 in transportation and distribution consol-
idated its ownership and control. And at once, arrayed
as solidly on the other side, were the 150,000 anthracite
miners. The bituminous mines, however, were not yet

28

consolidated; yet the 250,000 men employed therein were already combined. And not only that, but they were also combined with the anthracite miners, these 400,000 men being under the control and direction of one supreme labor council. And in this and the other great councils are to be found captains of labor of splendid abilities, who, in understanding of economic and industrial conditions, are undeniably the equals of their opponents, the captains of industry.

The United States is honeycombed with labor organizations. And the big federations which these go to compose aggregate millions of members, and in their various branches handle millions of dollars yearly. And not only this; for the international brotherhoods and unions are forming, and moneys for the aid of strikers pass back and forth across the seas. The Machinists, in their demand for a nine-hour day, affected 500,000 men in the United States, Mexico, and Canada. In England, the membership of working-class organizations is approximated by Keir Hardie at 2,500,000 with reserve funds $18,000,000. There the co-operative movement has a membership of 1,500,000, and every year turns over in distribution more than $100,000,000. In France, one-eigth of the whole working class is unionized. In Belgium the unions are very rich and powerful, and so able to defy the masters that many of the smaller manufacturers, unable to resist, *"are removing their works to other countries where the workmen's organizations are not so potent"*. And in all other countries, according to the stage of their economic and political development, like figures obtain. And Europe, to-day, confesses that her greatest social problem is the labor problem, and that it is the one most closely engrossing the attention of her statesmen.

The organization of labor is one of the chief acknowledged factors in the retrogression of British trade. The workers have become class conscious as never before. The wrong of one is the wrong of all. They

29

have come to realize, in a short-sighted way, that their
masters' interests are not their interests. The harder
they work, they believe, the more wealth they create for
their masters. Further, the more work they do in one
day, the fewer men will be needed to do the work. So the
unions place a day's stint upon their members, beyond
which they are not permitted to go. In "A Study of Trade
Unionism", by Benjamin Taylor in the <u>Nineteenth Century</u>
of April, 1898, are furnished some interesting corrobor-
ations. The facts here set forth were collected by the
Executive Board of the Employers' Federation, the document-
ary proofs of which are in the hands of the secretaries.
In a certain firm the union workmen made eight ammunition
boxes a day. Nor could they be persuaded into making more.
A young Swiss, who could not speak English, was set to
work, and in the first day he made fifty boxes. In the
same firm the skilled union hands filed up the outside
handles of one machine-gun a day. That was their stint.
No one was known ever to do more. A non-union filer came
into the shop and did twelve a day. A Manchester firm
found that to plane a large bed-casting took union workmen
one hundred and ninety hours, and non-union workmen one
hundred and thirty-five hours. In another instance a man,
resigning from his union, day by day did double the amount
of work he had done formerly. And to cap it all, an English
gentleman, going out to look at a wall being put up for
him by union bricklayers, found one of their number with
his right arm strapped to his body, doing all the work with
his left arm - forsooth, because he was such an energetic
fellow that otherwise he would involuntarily lay more
bricks than his union permitted.

     All England resounds to the cry, *"Wake up, England!"*
But the sulky giant is not stirred. *"Let England's trade
go to pot"*, he says; *"what have I to lose?"* And England
is powerless. The capacity of her workmen is represented
by 1, in comparison with the 2¼ capacity of the American
workman. And because of the solidarity of labor and the
destructiveness of strikes, British capitalists dare not
even strive to emulate the enterprise of American

capitalists. So England watches trade slipping through her fingers and wails unavailingly. As a correspondent writes: *"The enormous power of the trade unions hangs, a sullen cloud, over the whole industrial world here, affecting men and masters alike."*

The political movement known as Socialism is, perhaps, even less realized by the general public. The great strides it has taken and the portentious front it to-day exhibits are not comprehended; and, fastened though it is in every land, it is given little space by the capitalist press. For all its plea and passion and warmth, it wells upward like a great, cold tidal wave, irresistible, inexorable, ingulfing present-day society level by level. By its own preachment it is inexorable. Just as societies have sprung into existence, fulfilled their function, and passed away, it claims, just as surely is present society hastening on to its dissolution. This is a transition period -- and destined to be a very short one. Barely a century old, capitalism is ripening so rapidly that it can never live to see a second birthday. There is no hope for it, the Socialists say. It is doomed.

The cardinal tenet of Socialism is that forbidding doctrine, the materialistic conception of history. Men are not the masters of their souls. They are the puppets of great, blind forces. The lives they live and the deaths they die are compulsory. All social codes are but the reflexes of existing economic conditions, plus certain survivals of past economic conditions. The institutions men build they are compelled to build. Economic laws determine at any given time what these institutions shall be, how long they shall operate, and by what they shall be replaced. And so, through the economic process, the Socialist preaches the ripening of the capitalistic society and the coming of the new co-operative society.

The second great tenet of Socialism, itself a phase of the materialistic conception of history, is the class

struggle. In the social struggle for existence, men
are forced into classes. *"The history of all society
thus far is the history of class strife."* In the existing society the capitalist class exploits the working
class, the proletariat. The interests of the exploiter
are not the interests of the exploited. *"Profits are
legitimate"*, says the one. *"Profits are unpaid wages"*,
replies the other, when he has become conscious of his
class, *"therefore profits are robbery"*. The capitalist
enforces his profits because he is the legal owner because he controls the political machinery of society.
The Socialist sets to work to capture the political
machinery, so that he may make illegal the capitalist's
ownership of the means of production and make legal his
own ownership of the means of production. And it is
this struggle, between these two classes, upon which
the world has at last entered.

Scientific Socialism is very young. Only yesterday
it was in swaddling clothes. But to-day it is a vigorous
young giant, well braced to battle for what it wants,
and knowing precisely what it wants. It holds its international conventions, where world-policies are formulated
by the representatives of millions of Socialists. In
little Belgium there are three-quarters of a million
of men who work for the cause; in Germany, 3,000,000;
Austria, between 1895 and 1897, raised her socialist
vote from 90,000 to 750,000. France in 1871 had a
whole generation of Socialists wiped out; yet in 1885
there were 30,000, and in 1898 1,000,000.

Ere the last Spaniard evacuated Cuba, Socialist
groups were forming. And from far Japan, in these first
days of the twentieth century, writes on Tomoyoshi Murai:
*"The interest of our people in Socialism has been greatly
awakened these days, especially among our laboring people
on the one hand and young students' circle on the other,
as much as we can draw an earnest and enthusiastic aud-
ience and fill our hall, which holds two thousand...It*

*"is gratifying to say that we have a number of fine and
well-trained public orators among our leaders of Socialism in Japan. The first speaker tonight is Mr. Kiyoshi
Kawakami, editor of one of our city (Tokyo) dailies,
a strong, independent, and decidedly socialistic paper,
circulated far and wide. Mr. Kawakami is a scholar
as well as a popular writer. He is going to speak tonight on the subject, 'The Essence of Socialism – the
Fundamental Principles'. The next speaker is Professor
Iso Abe, president of our association, whose subject of
address is, 'Socialism and the Existing Social System'.
The third speaker is Mr. Naoe Kinosita, the editor of
another strong journal of the city. He speaks on the
subject, 'How to Realize the Socialist Ideals and
Plans'. Nextiis Mr. Shigeyoshi Sugiyama, a graduate of
Hartford Theological Seminary and an advocate of Social
Christianity, who is to speak on 'Socialism and Munifcal
Problems'. And the last speaker is the editor of the
'Labor World', the foremost leader of the labor-union
movement in our country, Mr. Sen Katayama, who speaks
on the subject, 'The Outlook of Socialism in Europe and
America'. These addresses are going to be published in
book form and to be distributed among our people to en-
lighten their minds on the subject."*

And in the struggle for the political machinery of
society, Socialism is no longer confined to mere propag-
anda. Italy, Austria, Belgium, England, have Socialist
members in their national bodies. Out of the one hundred
and thirty-two members of the London County Council,
ninety-one are denounced by the conservative element
as Socialists. The Emperor of Germany grows anxious
and angry at the increasing numbers which are returned
to the Reichstag. In France, many of the large cities,
such as Marseilles, are in the hands of the Socialists.
A large body of them is in the Chamber of Deputies, and
Millerand, Socialist, sits in the cabinet. Of him M.
Leroy-Beaulieu says with horror: *"M. Millerand is the
open enemy of private property, private capital, the
resolute advocate of the socialization of production..."*

33

"a constant incitement to violence...a collectivist, avowed and militant, taking part in the government, dominating the departments of commerce and industry, preparing all the laws and presiding at the passage of all measures which should be submitted to merchants and tradesmen."

In the United States there are already Socialist mayors of towns and members of State legislatures, a vast literature, and single Socialist papers with subscription lists running up into the hundreds of thousands. In 1896, 36,000 votes were cast for the Socialist candidate for President; in 1900, nearly 200,000; in 1904, 450,000. And the United States, young as it is, is ripening rapidly, and the Socialists claim, according to the materialistic conception of history, that the United States will be the first country in the world wherein the toilers will capture the political machinery and expropriate the bourgeoisie.

But the Socialist and labor movements have recently entered upon a new phase. There has been a remarkable change in attitude on both sides. For a long time the labor unions refrained from going in for political action. On the other hand, the Socialists claimed that without political action labor was powerless. And because of this there was much ill feeling between them, even open hostilities, and no concerted action. But now the Socialists grant that the labor movement has held up wages and decreased the hours of labor, and the labor unions find that political action is necessary. To-day both parties have drawn closely together in the common fight. In the United States this friendly feeling grows. The Socialist papers espouse the cause of labor, and the unions have opened their ears once more to the wiles of the Socialists. They are all leavened with Socialist workmen, "boring from within", and many of their leaders have already succumbed. In England, where class consciousness is more developed, the name "Unionism" has been replaced by "The New Unionism", the main object of which is *"to capture existing social structures in the interests of the wage-earners"*. There the Socialist, the trade-union, and other working-class organizations are beginning to co-operate in securing the return of representatives to the House of Commons. And in France, where the city councils and mayors of Marseilles and Monteaules-Mines are Socialistic, thousands of francs of municipal money were voted for the aid of the unions in the recent great strikes.

For centuries the world has been preparing for the coming of the common man. And the period of preparation virtually past, labor, conscious of itself and its desires, has begun a definite movement toward solidarity. It believes the time is not far distant when the historian will speak not only of the dark ages of feudalism, but of the dark ages of capitalism. And labor sincerely believes itself justified in this by the terrible indictment it brings against capitalistic society. In the face of its enormous wealth, capitalistic society forfeits its right to existence when it permits widespread, bestial poverty. The philosophy of the survival of the fittest does not soothe the class-conscious worker when he learns through his class literature that among the Italian pants-finishers of Chicago* the average weekly wage is $1.31, and the average number of weeks employed in the year is 27.85. Likewise when he reads:** *"Every room in these reeking tenements houses a family or two. In one room a missionary found a man ill with small-pox, his wife just recovering from her confinement,*

---

* From figures presented by Miss Nellie Mason Auten in the American Journal of Sociology, and copied extensively by the trade-union and Socialist press.

** "The Bitter Cry of Outcast London".

*"and the children running about half naked and covered
with dirt. Here are seven people living in one under-
ground kitchen, and a little dead child lying in the
same room. Here live a widow and her six children, two
of whom are ill with scarlet fever. In another, nine
brothers and sisters, from twenty-nine years of age
downward, live, eat, and sleep together."* And likewise,
when he reads:* *"When one man, fifty years old, who has
worked all his life, is compelled to beg a little money
to bury his dead baby, and another man, fifty years
old, can give ten million dollars to enable his daughter
to live in luxury and bolster up a decaying foreign aristocracy, do you see nothing amiss?"*

And on the other hand, the class-conscious worker
reads the statistics of the wealthy classes, knows what
their incomes are, and how they get them. True, down
all the past he has known his own material misery and
the material comfort of the dominant classes, and often
has this knowledge led him to intemperate acts and unwise
rebellion. But to-day, and for the first time, because
both society and he have evolved, he is beginning to see
a possible way out. His ears are opening to the propag-
anda of Socialism, the passionate gospel of the dispossess-
ed. But it does not inculcate a turning back. The way
through is the way out, he understands, and with this in
mind he draws up the programme.

It is quite simple, this programme. Everything is
moving in his direction, toward the day when he will
take charge. The trust? Ah, no. Unlike the trembling
middle-class man and the small capitalist, he sees nothing
for him to do but socialize distribution, and all is

---

* An item from the <u>Social Democratic Herald.</u> Hundreds
of these items, culled from current happenings, are
published weekly in the papers of the workers.

accomplished. The trust. *"It organizes industry on an enormous, labor-saving scale, and abolishes childish, wasteful competition."* It is a gigantic object lesson, and it preaches his political economy far more potently than he can preach it. He points to the trust, laughing scornfully in the face of the orthodox economists. *"You told me this thing could not be"**, he thunders. *"Behold, the thing is!"*

He sees competition in the realm of production passing away. wWhen the captains of industry have thoroughly organized production, and got everything running smoothly, it will be very easy for him to eliminate the profits by stepping in and having the thing run for himself. And the captain of industry, if he be good, may be given the privilege of continuing the management on a fair salary. The sixty millions of dividends which the Standard Oil Company annually declares will be distributed among the workers. The same with the United States Steel Corporation. The president of that corporation knows his business. Very good. Let him become Secretary of the Department and Steel of the United States. But since the chief executive of a nation of seventy-odd millions works for $50,000 a year, the Secretary of the Department of Iron and Steel must expect to have his salary cut accordingly. And not only will the workers take to themselves the profits of national and municipal monopolies, but also the immense revenues which the dominant classes to-day draw from rents, and mines, and factories, and all manner of enterprises.

All this would seem very like a dream, even to the worker, if it were not for the fact that like things have been done before. He points triumphantly to the aristocrat of the eighteenth century, who found, legislated, governed

---

* Karl Marx, the great Socialist, worked out the trust development forty years ago, for which he was laughed at by the orthodox economists.

37

and dominated society, but who was shorn of power and displaced by the rising bourgeoisie.. Ay, the thing was done, he holds. And it shall be done again, but this time it is the proletariat who does the shearing...Sociology has taught him that m - i - g - h - t spells "right". Every society has been ruled by classes, and the classes have ruled by sheer strength, and have been overthrown by sheer strength. The bourgeoisie, because it was the stronger, dragged down the nobility of the sword; and the proletariat, because it is the strongest of all, can and will drag down the bourgeoisie.

And in that day, for better or worse, the common man becomes the master - for better, he believes. It is his intention to make the sum of human happiness far greater. No man shall work for a bare living wage, which is degradation. Every man shall have work to do, and shall be paid exceedingly well for doing it. There shall be no slum classes, no beggars...Nor shall there be hundreds of thousands of men and women condemned, for economic reasons to lives of celibacy or sexual infertility. Every man shall be able to marry, to live in healthy, comfortable quarters, and to have all he wishes to eat as many times a day as he wishes. There shall no longer be a life-and-death struggle for food and shelter. The old heartless law of development shall be annulled.

All of which is very good and very fine. And when these things have come to pass, what then? Of old, by virtue of their weakness and inefficiency in the struggle for food and shelter, the race was purged of its weak and inefficient members. But this will no longer obtain. Under the new order the weak and the progeny of the weak will have a chance for survival equal to that of the strong and the progeny of the strong. This being so, the premium upon strength will have been withdrawn, and on the face of it the average strength of each generation, instead of continuing to rise, will begin to decline.

When the common man's day shall have arrived,
the new social institutions of that day will prevent the
weeding out of weakness and inefficiency. All, the
weak and the strong, will have an equal chance for pro-
creation. A nd the progeny of all, of the weak as well
as the strong, will have an equal chance for survival.
This being so, and if no new effective law of development be put into operation, then progress must cease.
And no only progress, for deterioration would at once
set in. It is a pregnant problem. What will be the
nature of this new and most necessary law of development?
Can the common man pause long enough from his under-
mining labors to answer? Since he is bent upon dragging
down the bourgeoisie and reconstructing society, can
he so reconstruct that a premium, in some unguessed way
or other, will still be laid upon the strong and efficient
so, that the human type will continue to develop? Can
the common man, or the uncommon men who are allied with
him, devise such a law? Or have they already devised
one? And if so, what is it?

******

www.ingramcontent.com/pod-product-compliance
Lightning Source LLC
Chambersburg PA
CBHW031444280326
41927CB00038B/1631